THE COUCH POTATO GUITAR WORKOUT

Technique-Building Exercises You Can Do While Watching TV!

GREG HORNE

Alfred, the leader in educational music publishing,

and the National Guitar Workshop,

one of America's finest guitar schools, have joined

forces to bring you the best, most progressive

educational tools possible. We hope you will enjoy

this book and encourage you to look for

other fine products from Alfred and the

National Guitar Workshop.

This book was acquired, edited, and produced
by Workshop Arts, Inc., the publishing arm of
the National Guitar Workshop.
Nathaniel Gunod, acquisitions, managing editor
Burgess Speed, acquisitions, senior editor
Timothy Phelps, interior design
Ante Gelo, music typesetter
Barbara Smolover, illustrator

Interior and cover photographs: © Paige M. Travis
Visit her blog: www.rocknrollsoapbox.com

Cover illustration: Stick Figure © iStockphoto.com / Toby Bridson

Alfred Music Publishing Co., Inc.
P.O. Box 10003
Van Nuys, CA 91410-0003
alfred.com

ISBN-10: 0-7390-6986-1
ISBN-13: 978-0-7390-6986-8

CONTENTS

ABOUT THE AUTHOR

Greg Horne is a guitarist, songwriter, author, and teacher in Knoxville, Tennessee. He is a senior faculty member of the National Guitar Workshop, and author of several books and DVDs published by National Guitar Workshop and Alfred, including the *Complete Acoustic Guitar Method, Teach Yourself Songwriting*, and two volumes of the *Complete Mandolin Method*. Greg holds a Bachelor of Arts in Music from the College of Wooster, and pursued graduate studies at the University of Mississippi.

Greg would like to thank Burgess Speed and Link Harnsberger for the great idea for this book. As a fan of both potatoes and couches, Greg does some of his practicing while watching reruns of '70s sitcoms and thinking about sweet potato fries.

To contact Greg, hear his music, and see his videos, please visit: www.greghornemusic.com

INTRODUCTION

Welcome to *The Couch Potato Guitar Workout*. This page has a lot of text on it, so you might want to read it while you're microwaving popcorn or something.

WHO IS THIS BOOK FOR?

Players of all levels—beginning to advanced—can benefit from the exercises and information in this book. It is helpful if you already know how to read standard notation or TAB, but if you do not, there is a review starting on page 6. It is also helpful if you already have a grasp of basic guitar technique. But if you don't, you will find plenty of helpful tips throughout.

HOW TO USE THIS BOOK

Mixed in with all the silliness in this book are good tips about how your hands work, how to practice, and how to achieve substantial improvement. The exercises in this book are meant to give you ideas that you can build on as your technique improves. It's an idea book. There isn't a set program of exercises to follow, because everybody has different problems to solve and different goals.

Exercises are solutions to problems. For the exercise to do any good, you have to know what problem you're trying to solve. You'll get the most benefit by using a small number of exercises and practicing them over the course of several sessions. Improvement will be gradual, and the process is helped by working on something for a while, letting it rest, and trying it again at the next session. Again, the "rest" part is important. When an exercise isn't showing positive results after a while, flip through the book and find a new one to add to the mix. Try to find things that relate to the other stuff you're practicing when you're not on the couch.

DO I HAVE TO USE A PICK? I LOST MINE IN THE COUCH...

This book is written from the perspective of playing with a pick, but the exercises can easily be adapted to fingerstyle and classical playing with great results. Just use these exercises as a starting point for different fingerpicking patterns and combinations.

IT'S ALL A TRICK, MWA-HA-HA-HA!

The truth is that you can't be totally mindless when you're practicing technique exercises. You have to pay attention to what you're doing, how you're doing it, and why you're doing it in the first place. At first, it would be smart to do your couch potato exercises during commercials with the sound off so you can really focus. After you get a repertoire of exercises mastered, you'll have a better technical foundation when you want to just zone out and shred.

The main thing is to build better playing habits, rather than add more bad habits. Listen to your tone, observe the feelings in your muscles and joints, stay relaxed, and try to make as good of a sound as you possibly can.

HIDDEN BENEFITS

Sitting on the couch ranks low on doctor-recommended methods of weight loss. Nevertheless, it just might be beneficial to grab your guitar and dash off a few finger twisters next time the pizza delivery commercial beckons you with its hypnotic, cheesy charms. An arpeggio learned is another pizza crisis averted.

HOW TO SIT ON A COUCH AND A FEW SAFETY TIPS

You would think this is the easy part, wouldn't you?

Seriously, though, most of us sit on couches as if the bones that hold us up had all turned into lo mein—not the best guitar playing position. Plus, couches are squishy. Your elbows and arms are probably going to bump into things like stacks of laundry, magazines, and that vacuum cleaner hose that got stuck behind the cushion.

If you're really hoping to get something out of the exercises in this book, clear yourself some space on the mothership. Get your guitar in a position that makes it easier to play, somewhat centered on the body with the headstock pointing more up than down. A strap may help, and you'll probably need to cinch it up higher than normal to do any good.

Get your arms, elbows, and hands into a position where they can move freely without having to bend your wrists at a sharp angle. You want to prevent repetitive stress injuries, which can sneak up on you when you're shredding your way through a cop show marathon.

If you're going to do some serious technique building (during commercials, of course), consider moving up to the edge of the sofa and sitting up straight with both feet on the floor. It will improve circulation, give you the most freedom of movement, and make it easier to reach that bag of microwave popcorn you forgot about yesterday.

Finally, if you must have your amp nearby, make sure it is stable and has plenty of ventilation. These exercises aren't that great for your neighbors to listen to anyway, so you'll save some fossil fuels and prevent fire risk by turning it off altogether. Besides, if it's too loud you won't hear who got voted off the pontoon boat in your favorite reality show.

Bad arm position and posture.

Good arm position and posture.

MUSIC NOTATION REVIEW

If you see something you don't understand in an example in this book, check the following two pages.

TABLATURE (TAB)

TAB (short for *tablature*) is the easiest way to read guitar music, though it leaves out some information about rhythm and expression. Here's what you might see on some TAB.

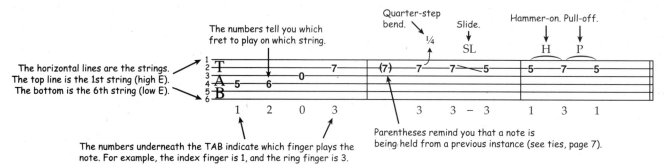

The numbers tell you which fret to play on which string.

Quarter-step bend.

Slide.

Hammer-on. Pull-off.

The horizontal lines are the strings.
The top line is the 1st string (high E).
The bottom is the 6th string (low E).

The numbers underneath the TAB indicate which finger plays the note. For example, the index finger is 1, and the ring finger is 3.

Parentheses remind you that a note is being held from a previous instance (see ties, page 7).

STANDARD MUSIC NOTATION

Standard music notation uses a *staff* of five horizontal lines to indicate *pitch* (the highness or lowness of a tone). Lower lines represent lower pitches. Notes are shown by oval *noteheads* o placed on lines, or in spaces between lines. Below are the basic notes on the staff. Notes are named "A" through "G."

The G clef, or treble clef, indicates that the second line from the bottom is the note G. It does this by encircling that line, crossing it four times.

Notes can be on lines or spaces.

E F G A B C D E F

In this book, standard music notation is directly above the TAB staff.

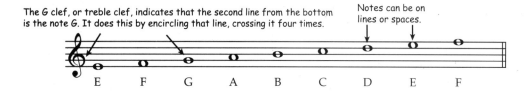

These are picking symbols:
⊓ is a *downstroke*
V is an *upstroke*.

The different note shapes indicate how long the notes last (see page 7).

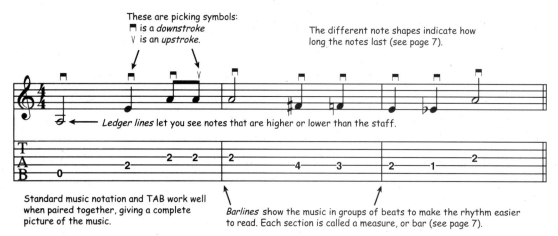

Ledger lines let you see notes that are higher or lower than the staff.

Standard music notation and TAB work well when paired together, giving a complete picture of the music.

Barlines show the music in groups of beats to make the rhythm easier to read. Each section is called a measure, or bar (see page 7).

ACCIDENTALS

Accidentals are symbols used to change the pitch of a note.

♯ is a *sharp*. It raises a note one *half step* (one fret). [1]

♭ is a *flat*. It lowers a note one half step.

A sharp or flat will last for the rest of the measure, unless a *natural* ♮ is used to return the note to its original pitch.

KEY SIGNATURES

Sharps or flats at the beginning of the staff are called the *key signature*. The key signature affects the indicated pitches in all octaves throughout the piece. To the right is the key signature for D Major, in which all F's and C's are sharped throughout.

Key signature

RHYTHM NOTATION

Rhythm in music is organized around the *beat*, which is the basic, steady pulse of a piece of music. Beats are grouped in *measures*, which are also called *bars*. Each measure has an equal number of beats. At the beginning of a piece of music is the *time signature*, which consists of two numbers, one stacked on top of the other. The top number shows how many beats will be in each measure. The bottom number shows what kind of note will equal one beat. This is commonly a 4, representing the quarter note. For instance, in the time signature to the right, there are four beats per measure, with the quarter note receiving one beat.

Time signature

Notes are shown with different shapes to indicate their *value,* or duration, in beats or fractions of beats. Periods of silence in music are indicated with *rests*. Following are the note shapes and rests with their durations.

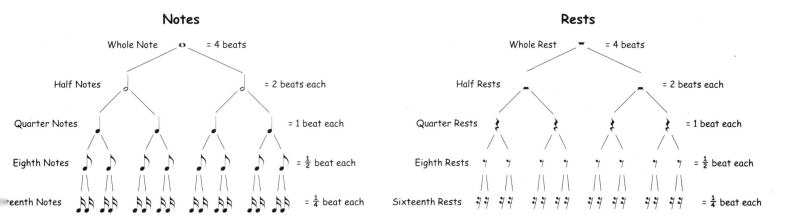

MORE RHYTHM SYMBOLS

A *dot* after a notehead increases the duration of the note by one half of its original value. This dotted half note lasts for 3 beats (2 + 1 = 3).

The left-facing repeat indicates a repeat of the passage of music. A right-facing repeat shows where to begin the repeated passage. If no right-facing repeat is shown, repeat from the beginning.

A *tie* connects two note values and makes them into one note lasting the duration of both. This note would last for 5 beats (4 + 1 = 5).

CHORD DIAGRAMS

Three or more notes played together is a *chord*. A *chord diagram* shows you the notes of a chord on the fretboard all at once. Following is a chord diagram and its features.

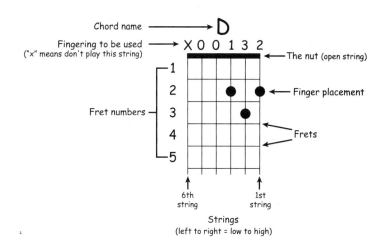

"SERIOUSLY, WHY DO YOU KEEP TWITCHING LIKE THAT?"— A LESSON IN FINGER MECHANICS

FLEXORS AND EXTENSORS

There are several different muscles that control finger movement. There are larger muscles in your forearm that connect to your fingers by tendons that travel through your wrist. There are also smaller muscles in your hand that control finer finger movements. This lesson concerns specific actions in the larger muscles of your forearm—*flexion*, *extension*, and the *twitch* response.

Flexors pull the finger toward the palm. *Extensors* straighten the finger out or lift the finger up. Imagine yourself typing—flexors press a key down, extensors lift the finger off the key.

TWITCHY, TWITCHY, TWITCHY

When you're first learning, you engage strong muscles that employ force and power to hold down the strings, like the kind you use to make and hold a fist. Remember those days?

With experience, just pressing down the strings becomes less of a big deal, and you're able to work on agility. This is where *fast twitch* muscle responses come into play. The fast twitch is used to move a body part to a new location quickly with a single impulse. Athletes such as runners train the fast twitch muscles in their legs to aid in sprints, for example.

For a musician, the twitch response makes all the difference in building agility while minimizing wear and tear (and possibly injury) to muscles and tendons. The first step is to identify the twitch so that you know what it feels like. Try the following:

1. **Achieve the resting point**
   Hold your fretting hand out in front of you, arm bent at the elbow as if you were looking at a wristwatch. Now, turn the back of your hand away from you about a quarter turn so you are looking at your thumb and index finger. Let the weight of your hand drop and relax, like you are floating in water. You are ready to get your flexor/extensor-twitch Kung Fu on. Take a deep breath, relax, and tune in to your body.

   First, observe that relaxed, floating-in-water state that your hand is hanging out in. This is the middle ground, the state of equilibrium between the flexors and extensors. It represents your finger when it is ready to play a note, but hasn't pressed down yet. This is the *resting point*.

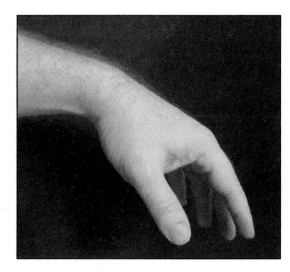

Resting point.

2. Do the flexor twitch

Twitch your index finger in toward your palm, as if you were scratching an itch just once. Your finger will travel a certain distance, beyond which you would have to engage other muscles to pull it all the way into your palm. We'll call this the *flexor twitch point*. Once you've twitched, you can either hold the finger in place at the twitch point (you might find it vibrates a little if you're really relaxed) or you can let it fall back to the resting point.

Twitch your index finger several times, letting it immediately fall back to the rest point. The movement should come from the knuckle where the finger joins the hand, not the joints further down the finger. This joint is called the *metacarpophalangeal* (or *MCP*) joint. If you're doing this right, you might actually feel the twitch ripple in the muscles of your forearm.

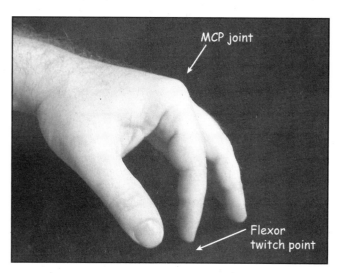

Flexor twitch point.

3. Do the extensor twitch

With your fingers in the resting point, try twitching your index finger the opposite direction, away from your palm. *Voila!* Extensor twitch! Let it fall back to the resting point. Try this twitch with other fingers. At first, you may have trouble isolating them. That's part of the process.

The extensor twitch is sometimes not as developed or practiced as the flexor twitch. Just remember that the extensor twitch is what gets your fretting finger off of a note and moving to the next one. It is just as important as the flexor twitch. Well-developed extensor responses can make the difference between a flurry of distinct notes and an unsynchronized mess.

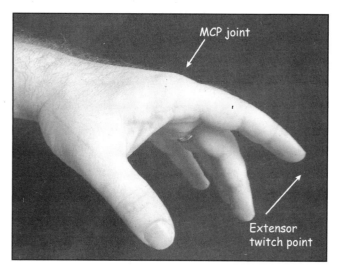

Extensor twitch point.

4. Try your other fingers

Congratulations, you have now isolated the flexor and extensor muscle twitch response. It's small, quick, and powerful. Try all your different fingers, even the fingers on your picking hand. If you are a fingerstyle player, you'll need those picking hand twitches just as much as the fretting ones.

You can practice isolating the twitch response anywhere anytime, without anybody really noticing too much. The more you practice it, the more control your brain has over those nerves and muscles. The ring finger and pinky need more practice than the others. Don't force these fingers to do things they can't do; just give them a little extra attention.

FINGER MECHANICS MAXIMIZERS (OR, HOW TO PRACTICE WITHOUT DRIVING YOUR COUCHMATE BANANAS)

Though it is hard to believe now, sometimes you will want to share your couch with other, non-guitar obsessed people. These people may not appreciate your desire to use every waking moment for the good of your guitar skills. They might just want to sit next to you and watch a movie or talk, or something like that. This kind of person is likely to fire you as their friend if they have to listen to hours of your "ticka-ticka-ticka" picking exercises every time they are trying to relax. Life is full of opportunities for compromise.

The good news is that a great deal of the value of practice consists of building the neural pathways that give your brain finer and more nimble control of your nervous system. Some of these pathways can be developed and strengthened even if someone has locked your guitar in the closet until you can learn to show some respect for the couch potato ways of others.

These "stealth" exercises can be done anywhere at any time. They work for both hands, even simultaneously. The thumb moves in a different direction than the fingers (hooray for opposable thumbs!), so use a little common sense in adapting these exercises to the thumb. Let it go the direction it wants to go.

STEALTH EXERCISE NO. 1: THE TELEGRAPH OPERATOR

In a "typing" position, rest your fingertips on your leg (or some other surface that allows your arm and shoulder to be relaxed). Your forearm and palm should be floating (not resting on the surface), and your wrist should be straight or arched slightly up. With all the other fingertips still touching the surface, raise and lower one finger in a typing motion. Repeat the motion 10 or 20 times before moving to the next finger. Start out slow and then go faster if you want.

TIPS: Stay relaxed! This exercise is for agility, not force. It's also about isolating the fingers so that you can move them without affecting the relaxation of the remaining fingers. You'll probably find this to be hardest with the ring finger, so be patient with that one.

STEALTH EXERCISE NO. 2: THE MINIATURE CHORUS LINE

Where the Telegraph Operator exercise mostly worked the flexors, this one works the extensors. Start in the same relaxed, resting-on-your-fingertips position. Start with the index finger, making a sudden, quick-fire kicking motion up in the air, while the other fingertips stay down. Think extensor twitch. Let the finger fall back down to the rest state, you don't need to bring it down with any force. Do this 10–20 times with each finger, and cycle through the fingers as much as you want.

STEALTH EXERCISE NO. 3: THE AMATEUR DANCE TEAM

This is a variation on the first two exercises where you attempt to do the exercise with two or three fingers together. If you're "typing," try to make the fingers contact the surface exactly at the same time, generating a single tapping sound. It's harder than it seems. You could also try this with the fingertips floating slightly above the surface.

STEALTH EXERCISE NO. 4: THE PENDULUM

Again, with your fingertips resting on the surface and your wrist arched up slightly, lift up the index finger and curl it in slightly so the finger doesn't touch the surface. Swing the finger forward and back like a pendulum (toward the palm, then away). If it helps you to imagine your swinging finger as a giant axe blade swinging in a graceful yet menacing manner over some hapless victim in an old horror movie, by all means do so. Try with each finger.

STEALTH EXERCISE NO. 5: THE VENUS FLYTRAP AND THE LEAPING TARANTULA

Hold your hand and arm so they are not resting on a surface, just relaxed and floating. Practice suddenly firing your flexor twitches all at once so that your fingers close on your palm fast like a Venus Flytrap (or like you're trying to clap with only one hand). Do this 10 times, then rest for 10 seconds. This and the following exercises are great for when you're warming up to practice or perform.

The extensor twitch version of the flytrap is the leaping tarantula. Starting from the resting state, suddenly extend your fingers from the MCP joint, then let them fall back to rest. It should look a little like a spider that has been disturbed and has used all its legs at once to spring into the air. Sleeping cats do this sort of thing in cartoons.

STRETCHING IS GOOD FOR YOU

Stretches can be done before you practice, during a break in practice, and after you're done. Below are a few good ones. Be gentle, go slow, and allow them to develop over time.

STRETCH NO. 1

Place your palms together in front of you, with the fingers and palms touching but not pressed hard together (see Fig. 1 below). First, bring your fingers together, then spread them apart several times while still touching each other (see Fig. 2 and Fig. 3). Then, keeping your fingers touching, very slowly and gently raise your elbows so that your palms gradually separate (see Fig. 4). Hold the stretch for 10 or 15 seconds, then slowly release and repeat. Don't force this stretch to go farther than you are comfortable with right away. Over time, as with any stretching exercise, your muscles will become more relaxed and limber.

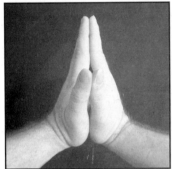
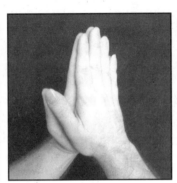
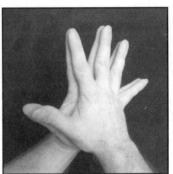

Fig. 1.   Fig. 2.   Fig. 3.   Fig. 4.

STRETCH NO. 2

Place the backs of your hands together in front of you, with the fingers hanging down. Slowly lower your elbows so that you feel a gentle stretch across the back of your wrists. Don't go too far. Hold for 10 or 15 seconds, slowly release, and repeat.

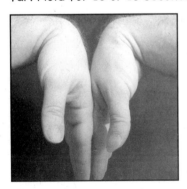

STRETCH NO. 3

You might need to stand up for this one. Hold your arms outstretched, parallel to the floor. Slowly make small circles with your arms going forward, and as you go, make the circles wider and wider. When your arms are almost vertical, begin making the circles smaller until you are back to the tiny circles you started with. Rest for a little while, then repeat with the circles going backward. This one is great for your shoulders and the circulation in your entire arm, which will improve the functioning of your fingers.

HEADROOM IS EVERYTHING

Imagine that your personal technique has three zones: Easy, Comfortably Challenging, and Redline. That redline zone is where things get uncomfortable and start to fall apart physically. It is the "ceiling" of your technique. Your goal with exercises and practice is to raise the ceiling, or to increase the *headroom* between the demands of the music you play and the ceiling of your ability to play. That headroom zone will be unique to the music and experience of each player. Here are a few simple guiding thoughts to keep in mind while practicing exercises.

THREE CONCEPTS THAT ARE ESSENTIAL TO HEADROOM

- **Accuracy**—A bunch of messy notes, when sped up, is a fast mess.
- **Synchronization** of right and left hand—The picking motion and the fretting motion need to be coordinated perfectly, or else you get missed notes.
- **Relaxation**—Learning to play without effort actually takes some effort. You have to think about and practice relaxing while you play.

Following are a few tips on the right and wrong approaches to practicing and increasing headroom.

THE WRONG WAY	THE RIGHT WAY
Practice incessantly, feel the burn.	Take breaks. Rest helps newly acquired skills become muscle memories (repeatable motions that don't have to be planned ahead).
Power through the pain.	Respond to pain by backing off, relaxing, taking a break, and examining your position to find the source of the problem. Reduce stress on your muscles, tendons, and joints whenever possible.
To play fa ster and faster, tighten up and force your way through.	Gradually, over a period of time, raise the speed at which you are able to play and still be relaxed.
Twist yourself into whatever position gets the job done.	Work on playing from as natural and relaxed a position as possible. Try to eliminate sharp bends in the wrist and arm, and tension in the neck and shoulders.
Move your pick fast and your fingers fast, and one day it will come together.	Get your synchronization of right and left hands together first. Make good, clear tones while playing slowly, and try to maintain clarity and accuracy as the tempo increases.

THE MOTHER OF ALL MINDLESS FRETBOARD EXERCISES

Here it is. It's as easy as one, two, three, four. Start at the first position (1st finger, 1st fret) on the 6th string. When you finish on the 1st string, move up one fret position and begin again, working from the 1st string back to the 6th. Keep going until you get up to the 9th position (4th finger playing the 12th fret). You can keep going beyond this point if you want.

Learn this exercise using steady quarter notes played with downstrokes. It helps if you count the quarter notes out loud: "One, Two, Three, Four."

Once you get this exercise all coordinated and can do it without having to stop and think about where to go next, it's time to bring in the *metronome!* This is an adjustable time-keeping device that clicks at a steady tempo. If you don't have a metronome, get one, or get a metronome software app for the computer device of your choice.

THE "GOLDILOCKS" PRINCIPLE APPLIED TO SPEED BUILDING

In the kids' story of *Goldilocks and the Three Bears,* the fickle young diva Goldilocks tries three chairs. One is too hard, one is too soft, and one is just right. With that in mind, here's a three-stage approach to speed building using your trusty metronome.

1. **Practice too slow.** Set the metronome at a very slow speed and work on the exercise while focusing on timing, relaxation, and tone. Create the best sounding notes you can at this stage.

2. **Practice too fast.** Find the highest metronome speed that still allows you to play the exercise perfectly. This is your *best fast speed.* For a short period of time, a few minutes or so, set the metronome a few clicks higher than your best fast speed. You won't be able to keep up perfectly, just relax and do the best you can. The purpose of this is to condition your brain to send the "playing instructions" to your muscles at a faster rate. It's okay if you don't have it perfect after a few minutes. Don't do this too long, or you may stress your muscles.

3. **Practice just right.** After you've practiced too fast for a little while, stop and rest a minute or so. Then dial the metronome back to the best fast speed you started with. Now, when you play at this speed, it should feel easier and more effortless than it did before. Gradually, over a period of days (or weeks or months), you'll find that your best fast speed keeps creeping its way up the metronome dial. Be patient. Your headroom is increasing!

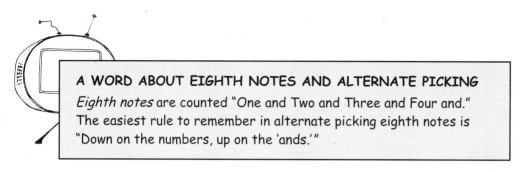

A WORD ABOUT EIGHTH NOTES AND ALTERNATE PICKING

Eighth notes are counted "One and Two and Three and Four and."
The easiest rule to remember in alternate picking eighth notes is
"Down on the numbers, up on the 'ands.'"

If you can do the basic exercise perfectly and easily using quarter notes with downstrokes, it's
time to add upstrokes. Try this version with each note doubled in eighth notes.

When you can work your way up the neck using double eighth notes, start doing the exercise
with single eighth notes (still alternate picking).

WHAT ASCENDS MUST DESCEND

Here's what the exercise looks like when you start on the 4th finger and descend. Start up high
on the neck, and work your way down one position at a time.

THE ON/OFF SWITCH: WORKING YOUR FLEXORS AND EXTENSORS

In this section, we'll look at some exercises to help you hone your flexor and extensor twitch responses. The goal here is to play notes with as little extraneous movement as possible and to learn to operate each finger without all the other fingers going all "crazy dance team competition" on you. This is actually one big exercise that's split up into pieces so you can get the motions down.

WORKING THE 2ND FINGER FLEXOR AND EXTENSOR

For the first piece, you will hold the 1st finger down on the 1st fret while your 2nd finger frets and releases the 2nd fret note. Keep in mind that you are working the twitch responses of the 2nd finger here, so concentrate only on the finger that's doing the work. Fretting works the flexor, releasing works the extensor. Try to be as robot-like as possible, this is mechanical stuff.

WORKING THE 3RD AND 4TH FINGER FLEXORS AND EXTENSORS

The following exercises will work the 3rd and 4th finger. The 1st finger is already well developed in this area, so we're not going to give it a specific exercise.

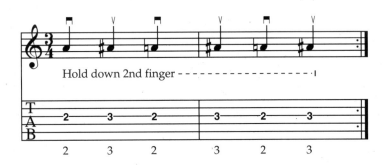

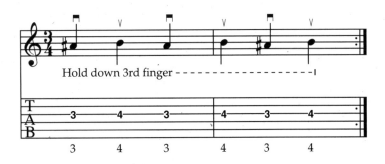

WE'LL BE BACK AFTER THIS WORD ABOUT TIME SIGNATURES

In this book, you'll see several different time signatures used, which allow the meter to adapt to the needs of the exercise. Often, the time signature will have a 4 on the bottom, indicating that each quarter note is one beat. The time signature $\frac{4}{4}$ has four quarter notes per bar, $\frac{3}{4}$ has three quarter notes, and $\frac{6}{4}$ has six quarter notes.

If the time signature has an 8 on the bottom, the top number will be a multiple of 3 (as in $\frac{6}{8}$, $\frac{9}{8}$, $\frac{12}{8}$). These meters group the eighth notes into groups of three, like *triplets* (three notes in the time of two). Each "triplet" is felt as one pulse, or beat. For example, the $\frac{9}{8}$ example shown below is felt as three beats of eighth-note triplets. $\frac{6}{8}$ would be felt as two beats of triplets, and $\frac{12}{8}$ would be felt as four beats of triplets.

Here's the big exercise with all the components put together, ascending the neck on the 3rd string. Try it on other strings, too. Remember to hold down the 1st finger while you're working the 2nd finger, and so on. This is not a speed exercise so go slow, and concentrate on accuracy, economy, and synchronization.

Note that your picking will alternate throughout, so each new beat and bar begin with a different pick direction. It may help to emphasize the beats by accenting them with your pick. Play the first note of each triplet group a little louder than the others. (See accenting tip on page 23.)

The on/off machine exercise going up the neck

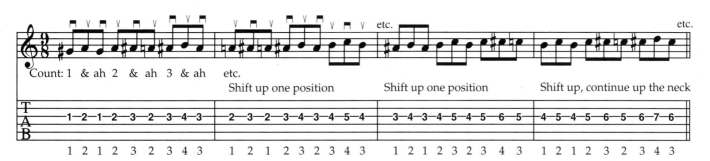

Here's what it looks like coming back down the neck.

The on/off machine exercise descending from the 12th fret

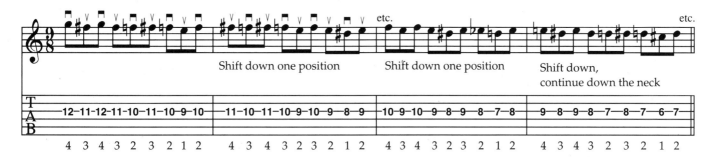

And now, back to your regularly scheduled program...

NOT THE WEAKEST LINK: GIVING EXTRA ATTENTION TO YOUR WEAKER FINGERS

Are your 3rd and 4th fingers weak and puny? Do they get made fun of at parties? You need these two exercises to give them a little extra workout so they can catch up to the others. The first one starts at the 12th fret and works down the neck.

The next one's tricky. It starts in the first position, then shifts up in the last two notes of each bar. Watch out for the rhythm; this one's in "triplets."

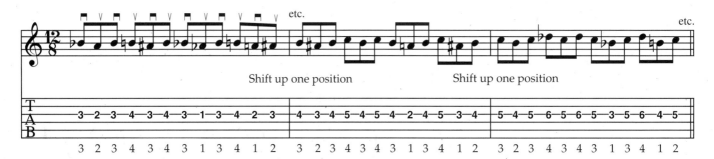

THE "IT SOUNDS LIKE YOU'RE REALLY DOING SOMETHING" TRICK

One of the great "sleight-of-hand" tricks guitar players use involves playing a melodic pattern on one string and alternating notes with the open string. You can hear this in every style, from AC/DC's "Thunderstruck" to bluegrass guitar solos. Not only is this a way to sound like you're doing something more impressive than you are, it's a great way to work on your flexor/extensor twitches and your pick synchronization. If your fingers don't get on and off the notes with perfect timing, it turns into a mess!

To start, get familiar with this B Major scale on the 2nd string.

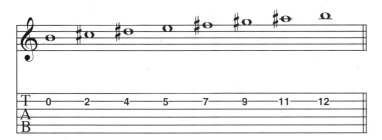

Below is a pattern that creates the outline of a chord progression. Note that the B Major scale has an A sharp, but this pattern has an A natural, which, if you're scoring at home, implies a B7 chord.

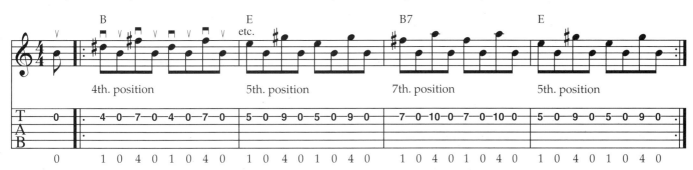

Here's one that has you using all four fingers and doing some position jumping.

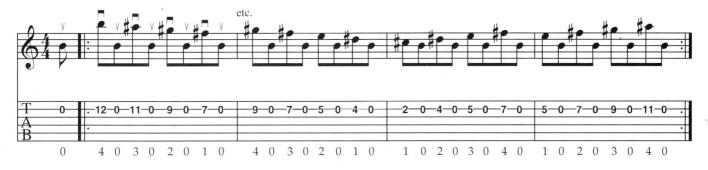

This one abandons the major scale and sounds sort of "metal" if you speed it up.

THE ROGUE FINGER: ADDING STRING CROSSING TO THE MOTHER OF ALL MINDLESS FRETBOARD EXERCISES

This is a set of exercises based on the old 1-2-3-4 exercises you learned so long ago (page 14). The challenge here is to displace one finger in the pattern to the next string, so that your pick and fingers get some practice crossing back and forth on adjacent strings. These are tricky at first, but they sound cool when you get them going. Once they can be easily played as written, practice them with eighth notes and alternate picking.

Be sure to practice your exercises with *legato* phrasing. The Italian musical term *legato* indicates that each note endures until the next note is sounded, so that the sound is not interrupted as you go from note to note. The opposite of *legato* is *staccato*, meaning the notes are played short and detached with a bit of silence between them.

Displacing Finger 2—Ascending

Displacing Finger 2—Descending

Displacing Finger 3—Ascending

Displacing Finger 3—Descending

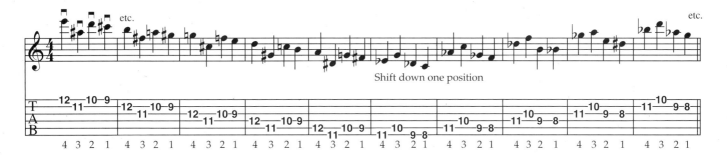

Displacing Finger 4—Ascending

There are two approaches you could use on the 4th finger displacement while descending. Try them both.

Displacing Finger 4—Descending (Version 1)

Displacing Finger 4—Descending (Version 2)

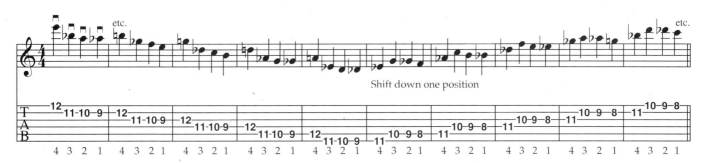

CONFUSE THE PICK: WORKING IN THREES

One of the best ways to develop your alternate picking agility is to practice three notes per string. This causes the pick direction of the first note to change each time you change strings. These exercises cover all of the three-finger combinations, ascending as you work from string 6 to string 1, then descending as you work back from string 1 to 6 (after a position shift).

Fingers 1-2-3

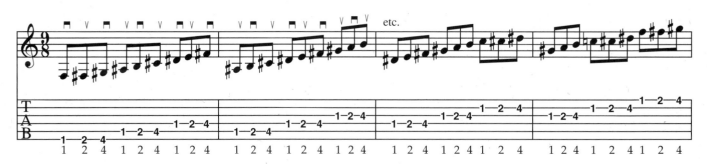

Fingers 1-2-4

TIP: As you get better at these exercises, practice *accenting* the first note of each triplet. To accent a note, you emphasize it by playing it louder than the others. Give yourself a little dynamic room for accents by playing most of the notes at a medium volume. You could also practice accenting other parts of the beat. The symbol indicating an accent is >.

Fingers 1-3-4

Fingers 2-3-4

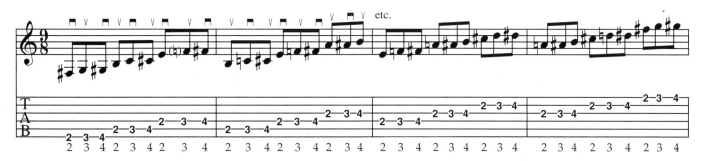

HAMMER-ONS AND PULL-OFFS

You've been very picky so far. It's time to smooth things out with *slurs*. In music, a *slur* indicates that one note leads to the next without a distinct new articulation of the second note (such as a pick attack). On the guitar, we make slurs by using *hammer-ons* and *pull-offs*. They are shown in music with an arc ⌒ connecting two notes, and in TAB with an H for hammer-on and P for pull-off.

Here's an exercise to warm up your hammer-ons going up the neck. To execute a hammer-on, play a note and then forcefully bring down a left-hand finger onto a higher note on the same string, thereby causing the second note to sound.

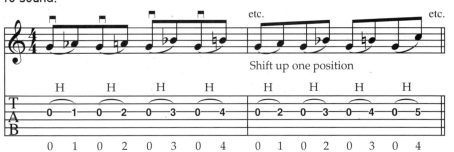

This one covers pull-offs. To execute a pull-off, play a note and the pull off (pull down, really) of the string so that a lower, already fretted note or open string is sounded.

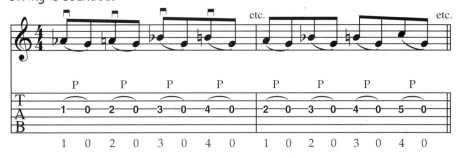

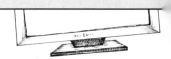

TIPS FOR BETTER H'S AND P'S

1. A good hammer-on is all about follow-through. Don't hesitate, or stop the downward motion of your finger too soon; imagine your finger is going to keep going all the way through the string to the wood of the fingerboard.

2. A good pull-off requires the finger making the pull-off to snap off the string in a plucking motion. If you just lift straight up, you won't hear the slurred note.

3. Listen to the sound you make. If you can't hear each hammer-on or pull-off note loud and clear, go back and give it some more work.

The next two exercises cover all the possible hammer-ons and pull-offs (except the 1st finger). The A exercise lets you repeat each move, then the B exercise condenses it all into one bar.

Hammer-Ons

Pull-Offs

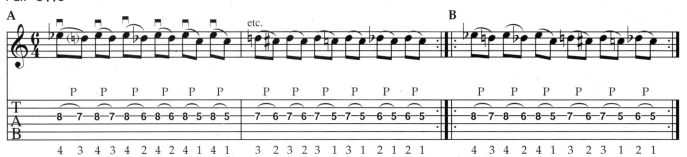

TAKE A TRILL RIDE

Below, you'll be working out the skills you need to play longer slurred phrases and *trills* (fast alternations between two notes). Notice that the pick hits only once per bar. This should allow you almost enough time to reach for a potato chip before the next bar. Try this exercise on different strings and in different spots on the neck. Make sure you can hear all the notes!

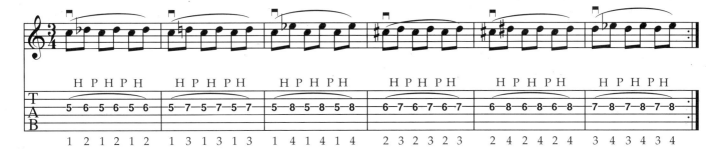

NOW IN TRIPLE STRENGTH FORMULA

The next exercise will help you work out in triplets. You'll pick the first note of the triplet, then hammer-on or pull-off the next two. Every three-finger combination is represented. The exercise is shown on the 3rd string at 5th position, but you can move it around to other positions for variety.

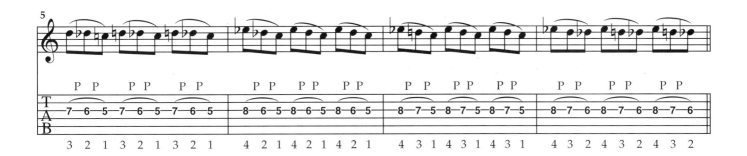

FACE-MELTING "WHEEDLY WHEEDLY" LICKS

Let's not hold back here: one of the best uses of repetitive practice time is building an arsenal of those thrilling, insistently repetitive lead guitar licks that drive crowds crazy. These are the licks that go "wheedly wheedly wheedly" and then usually end in a big bend and maybe some fireworks or lasers. They are fairly simple, but it takes a lot of practice to get them to flow smoothly and effortlessly. The next four pages are devoted to these licks.

A QUESTION FROM OUR STUDIO AUDIENCE: WHY SO MANY LICKS IN C♯ MINOR?
Many of these licks are shown in C♯ Minor because they are in the 9th position. This allows you to use the 9th fret and 12th fret dots as guides. It's high enough to sound right, but still reachable on an acoustic guitar if that's what you're playing. You're free to move these licks to any key or position you like.

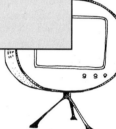

To start, here's a set of four triplet licks in different positions. These don't have to be super fast to sound good, just keep the beat steady and even. These kinds of licks can be heard in "All Right Now" by Free.

The "Wheedly" Triplet Starter Kit

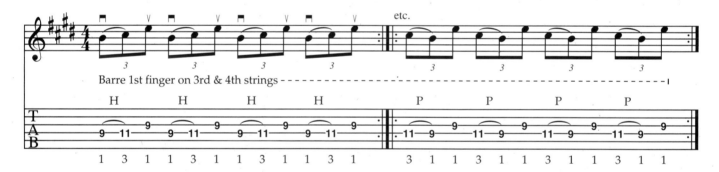

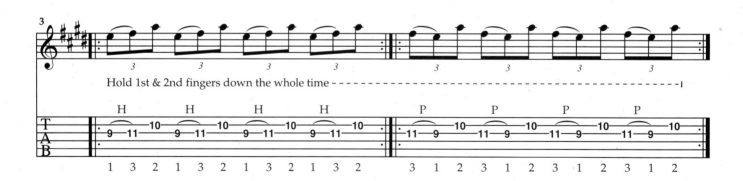

This set features the multiple pull-off sounds heard on rockabilly records in the 1950s (which, in turn, influenced the face-melting licks of the British rock scene in the 1960s and '70s). The bracket in the TAB shows the basic figure, which is then duplicated in cookie-cutter fashion for the rest of the bar.

Rockabilly Pull-Off Triplets (C♯ Minor)

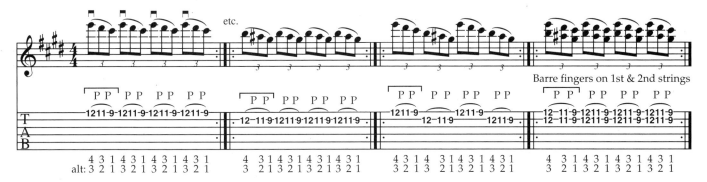

Here's a set of easy pull-off triplets you might hear on a Led Zeppelin record (or four). Since the pull-off is doing the work, it's fairly easy to get these going up to high RPM levels.

British Blues-Rock Pull-Off Triplets (C♯ Minor)

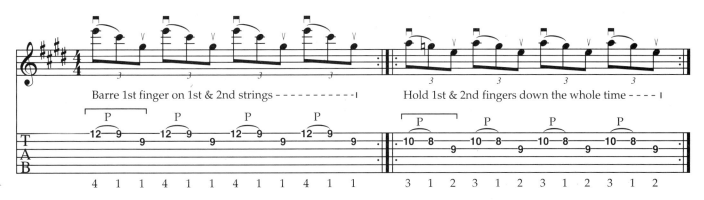

Add an extra note to the previous triplets with a hammer-on, and you've got four-notes-per-beat (sixteenths). That's a substantial increase in face-melting power for minimal effort!

British-Style Face-Melting Sixteenths (C♯ Minor)

Here are some licks that give tribute to the more pop-oriented sounds in the classic rock canon. The first one is reminiscent of Mark Knopfler's brilliant solo on Dire Straits' "Sultans of Swing." Knopfler played his version without a pick, instead using his thumb, index, and middle fingers in a rolling pattern.

The Sultan's Whirling Dervish (C# Minor)

Here's a lick that begins with fast-picked notes and accelerates into very fast pull-offs. A lick like this appears in a famous Journey song that addresses the following age-old conundrum: *To stop believin', or not to stop believin'; that is the question.*

"Gas Pedal" Accelerating Lick (A Major)

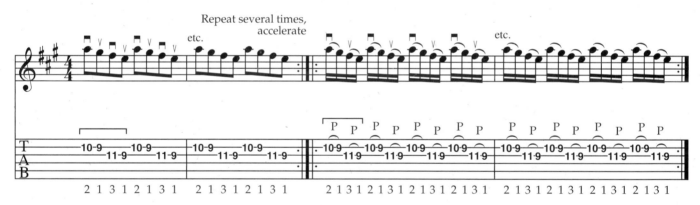

This one has a lot of chord motion that is good for your Heart.

Crazy Chord Triplets

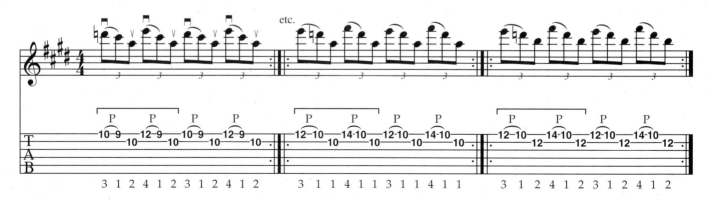

Here are a bunch of face-melting licks that lead off from a bend using the 3rd finger. This bend should push up towards your head, rather than pull down towards your feet. This is because the notes that follow the bend are often on a higher string. It's also very wise to use your 2nd finger on the same string as your 3rd finger to help out with the bend. This first set is inspired by Chuck Berry.

Rockin' Blues Benders (C# Minor)

The following set has the stuttering sound of a needle stuck in a vinyl record groove, repeating the same thing over and over. Digital downloads don't have this feature.

Vinyl Skipping Bends (C# Minor)

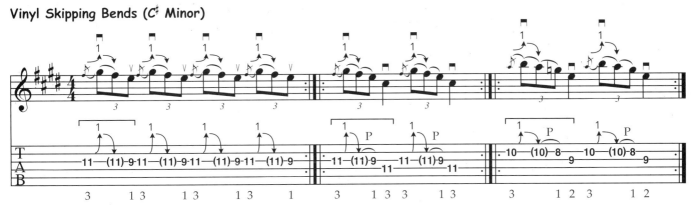

The last two are even more jagged and asymmetrical sounding. These kinds of licks don't really have to line up to the beat in a song. Instead, they kind of roll over the beat on their own inertia until they hit a wall and blow up (and the crowd goes wild). *Sextuplet* rhythms are featured in the second example. A sextuplet is six notes in the time of four (in this case, four sixteenth notes and an eighth note in the time of four sixteenth notes, or one beat).

Bendy Face-Melters (C# Minor)

Sextuplets of Rock (C# Minor)

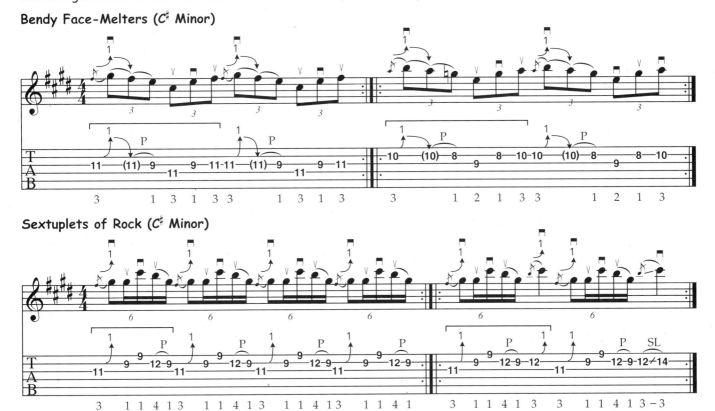

SCALES (A FISHY SUBJECT)

There's not room in this book to teach you all about scales and how to use them. But, if you know a scale or two, here are some ideas on getting the most out of them during mindless couch potato practicing time. For these exercises, you're going to use a C Major scale. You could adapt these exercises to any key or type of scale you wish—they're just patterns.

Below is a C Major scale. The major scale is made by starting on the *key note* (the note the scale is named after, in this case C) and following this pattern of whole steps and half steps: Whole–Whole–Half–Whole–Whole–Whole–Half. The following C Major scale begins with finger 2 on string 6 at the 8th fret, which places it in 7th position.

C Major Scale (7th Position, Starting on Finger 2)

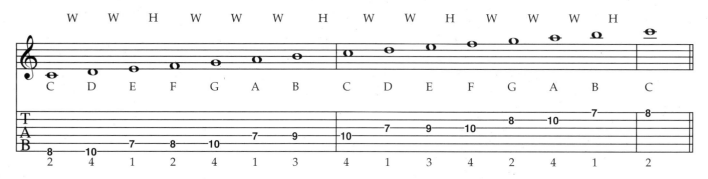

And now, let's play a bunch of patterns. In the first one, you follow this pattern: skip up a *3rd* (every other scale step is an *interval,* or distance, of a 3rd), go down a step, skip up a 3rd, go down a step, etc.

Ascending: Up a 3rd, Down a Step

Here's the descending version of the pattern.

Descending: Down a 3rd, Up a Step

The following patterns are called *sequences*. A sequence is a short pattern of notes that is duplicated starting on the next scale step up (or down). Sequences are used heavily in classical music (composer J.S. Bach was a big fan of them during the Baroque era). They are also used in shredding guitar solos to help get maximum notage out of a small set of notes. If you are using a pattern and then "rubber stamping" it up the scale, you don't run out of notes as fast. In the first bar of the following examples, the brackets in the TAB will help you see the initial pattern; the bars that follow show the sequences moving up the scale.

Sequence: Up Three Steps and Down a 3rd

These sequences are written in sixteenth notes, but that doesn't mean they have to be fast. It just means you've got four notes per beat. Below is another pattern. Once you've got it, just reverse the pattern to come down from the top note. Be sure to alternate your picking!

Sequence: Up Four Steps and Down a 3rd

The next one's in triplets to challenge your picking. It helps at first to accent the first note of each triplet with your pick so you can feel the three notes per beat. Don't forget to try it descending.

Triplet Sequence: Up Two Steps and Down One Step

AN ARPEGGIO IS NOT A STRING OF ISLANDS

That would be an *archipelago*, which you would know if you watched the science channel instead of those reality shows you love so much. An *arpeggio* is a chord that has been broken up so each note is played separately. Arpeggio exercises are great for the improvement of your alternate picking and your knowledge of the guitar neck.

There are a couple of different ways to tackle arpeggios on the guitar. The first way is by using a chord position that stays in one place (as if you were going to strum it) and playing all the notes separately. This method is best for challenging your cross-string alternate picking and for playing chord progressions. Some examples of this kind of playing would include the guitar parts to Lynyrd Skynyrd's "Simple Man," The Who's "Behind Blue Eyes," and Merle Haggard's "Mama Tried."

These exercises are designed to give you some ideas of picking patterns to try. Your goals are clean notes, even tone, and alternate picking. This first one features a cool E Minor progression that would be fun to play while you're watching a cop show. Try it with other chords, too.

E Minor Arpeggio Progression

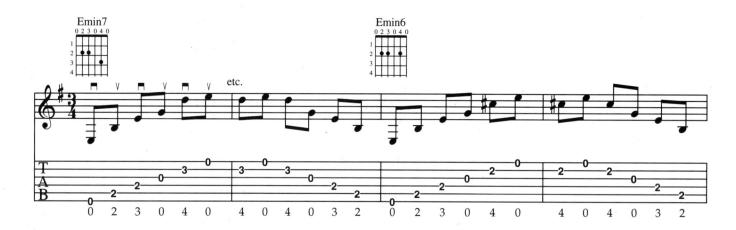

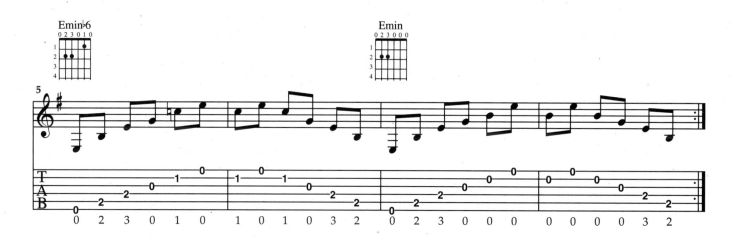

The next one involves skipping a string with your pick. To keep the rhythm even, you have to double up a couple of notes in the Cadd9 chord because you're working with fewer strings.

Skipping a String

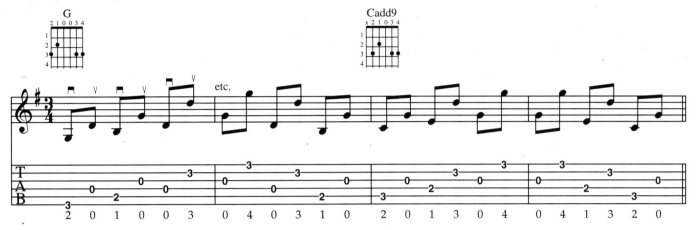

This one is sort of like a banjo-style roll. Be careful with your alternate picking!

Descending Three-String Pattern

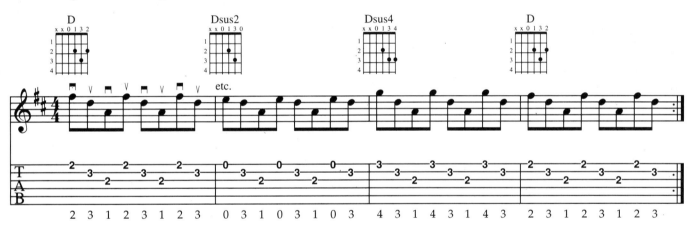

In this one, the bass note moves to different strings, while the chord remains on the first three strings.

Moving Bass Note Progression

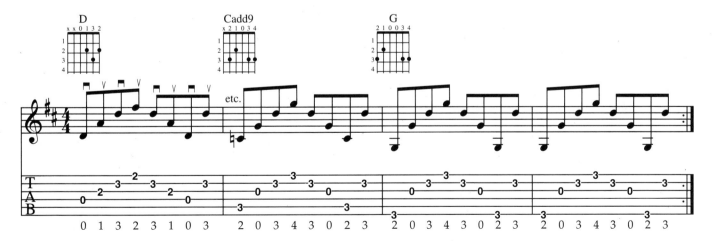

ARPEGGIOS PART DEUX: THE REAL ARPEGGIOS

The exercises you played on the previous page were really cross-string chord-picking patterns. To play "real" arpeggios that include all the notes of a chord in order, you need to know something about how chords are constructed.

MAJOR TRIAD

To the right is an A Major triad (a three-note chord). It contains a root (A), a 3rd (C♯), and a 5th (E), which correspond to the 1st, 3rd, and 5th notes of an A Major scale.

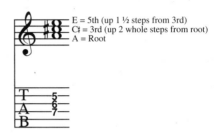

MINOR TRIAD

To the right is an A Minor triad. To make a minor triad, you lower the 3rd of a major triad by one half step (which is then referred to as the ♭3rd, or "flat 3rd.")

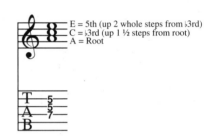

The following exercises work with true arpeggios that include all of the roots, 3rds, and 5ths of the triads. These arpeggios can help you learn the neck by showing you an outline of all the chord tones for a particular chord. On the guitar, there are many ways to finger a given arpeggio. Here are some good fingerings for A Major and D Major triads, starting on different fingers. You can move them around the neck to find other chords. For instance, if you move the first example up a fret, so that the root is on B♭, you would have a B♭ Major arpeggio.

* = Shift position

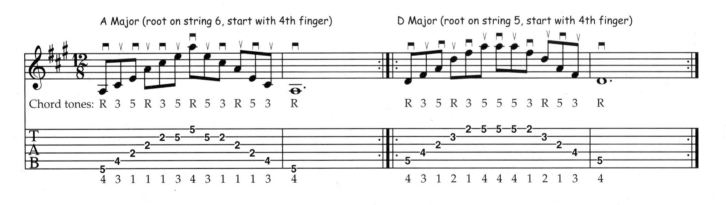

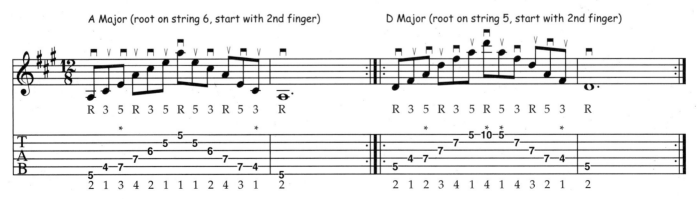

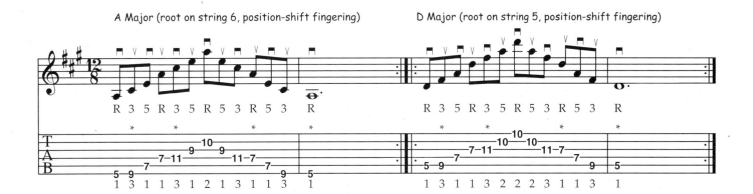

A Major (root on string 6, position-shift fingering)   D Major (root on string 5, position-shift fingering)

Following are some good fingerings for A Minor and D Minor arpeggios. You can use the major fingerings and the minor fingerings as starting points to figure out arpeggios for other major and minor chords on the neck. For example, to find a B Minor arpeggio, you could move the A Minor fingerings up one whole step.

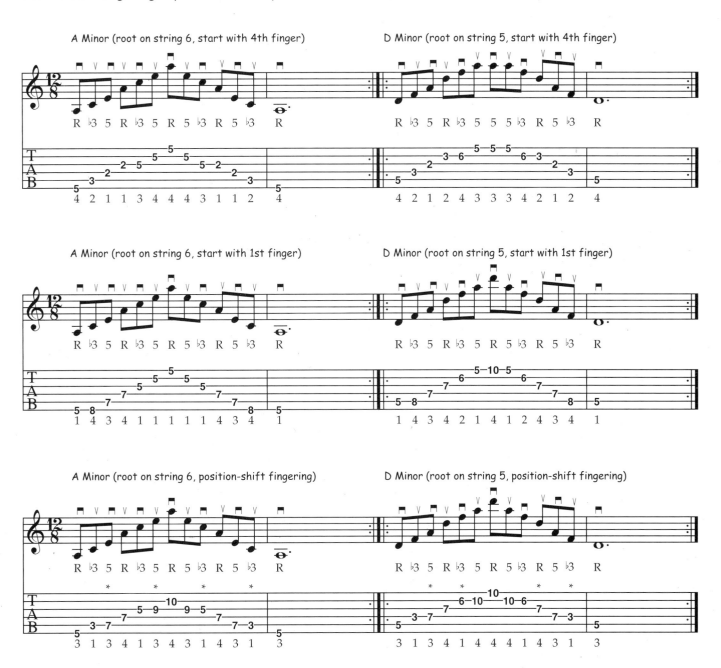

A Minor (root on string 6, start with 4th finger)   D Minor (root on string 5, start with 4th finger)

A Minor (root on string 6, start with 1st finger)   D Minor (root on string 5, start with 1st finger)

A Minor (root on string 6, position-shift fingering)   D Minor (root on string 5, position-shift fingering)

HYBRID PICKING (OR, HOW TO PUT THOSE LAZY, GOOD-FOR-NOTHING PICKING-HAND FINGERS TO WORK—FOR FUN AND PROFIT)

If you've been playing the exercises in this book with a pick, then the remaining fingers of your picking hand have not been seeing much action (unless you use them to hold on to your potato chips while you're picking).

Since you're on the couch anyway, why not pick up a new technique? *Hybrid picking* is the term for playing with a flatpick and a couple of picking-hand fingers at the same time. It's used by country pickers, blues wailers, and rock shredders.

Usually, hybrid picking is done in a three-string group. For example, if you're dealing with strings 2, 3, and 4, the pick plays string 4, the middle finger (*m*) plays string 3, and the ring finger (*a*) plays string 2. A three-string group is sometimes referred to as a "grab." You can move the grab to whatever set of three strings you want to play.

All of the following exercises use the same A Major chord on strings 2, 3, and 4. Once you've got the patterns down, try them on any chord, or group of strings, you like. Here's a starter set of patterns where the pick plays alone and the fingers play together. Each bar is a separate exercise, so you don't have to play them in a row. In the third bar, the pick even begins to alternate.

"Pick and Pinch" Exercises

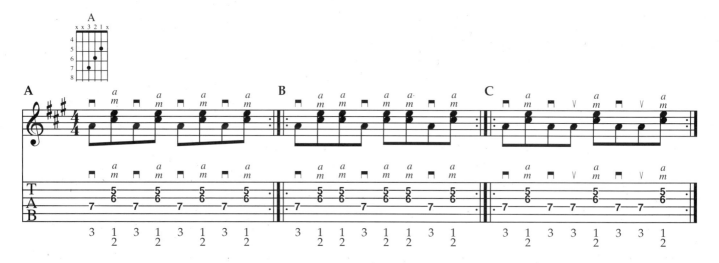

Now, we're going to try some banjo-style patterns called "rolls." There are forward rolls, backward rolls, and alternating rolls. Below is the forward roll, with each pattern leading from a different note. You can play these separately or as one long roll (without the repeats).

Forward Rolls

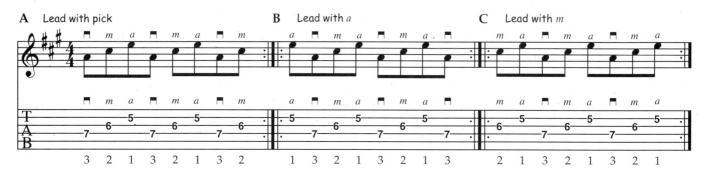

Here are the backward rolls, again leading from different notes.

Backward Rolls

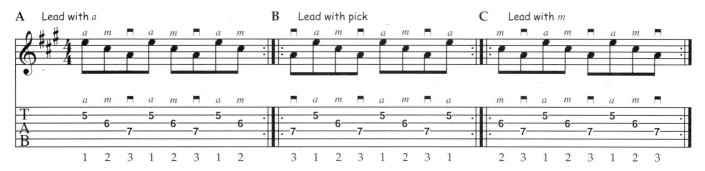

This set of exercises shows you the various possibilities for alternating rolls. Try them one at a time—they are more challenging than they look.

Alternating Rolls

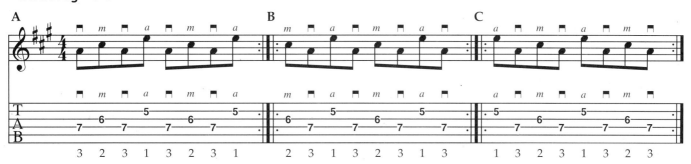

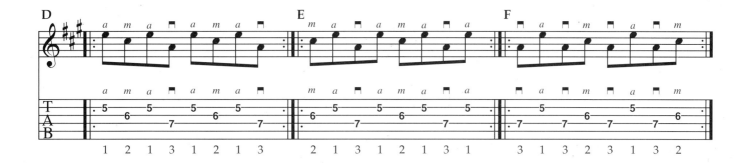

Once you've worked up the rolls, start combining them and moving them around. Here's a combination roll that goes "forward, forward, forward, back, back, back." Exercise A stays on three strings, while Exercise B moves to new strings.

Combination Forward-Backward Roll

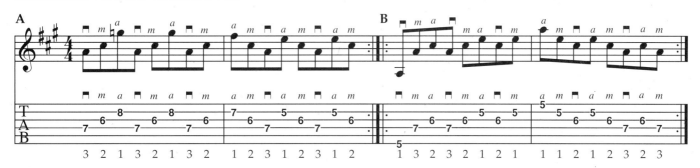

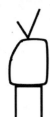

GET UP AND MOW THE LAWN! JUST KIDDING, MORE MINDLESS FINGER-TWISTERS

Here's a challenging one. Take the "Mother of All Mindless Fretboard Exercises" and replace one note on each string with a rest. First, you'll rest on the 2nd note on string 6, then on the 3rd note on string 5, the 4th note on string 4, no notes on string 3, the 1st note on string 1. Confused?

The Wandering Rest

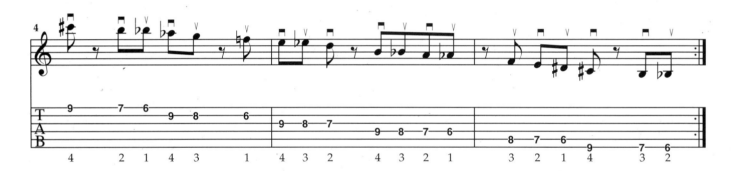

The next one works on your stretch between the 1st and 4th fingers. Notice how you "inch" your way down the fretboard.

The Inchworm

* = Shift position

THE CHROMATIC SCALE, BECAUSE YOU NEVER KNOW WHEN YOU'RE GOING TO NEED ALL 12 NOTES

Following are some exercises for practicing the *chromatic scale,* which is a scale made up of all 12 half steps within an octave. There are two fingerings shown below. The first fingering uses four notes per string but requires you to shift positions every time you change to a new string (except for the 2nd string). The second fingering uses five notes per string. You either play two notes with the 4th finger or two notes with the 1st finger.

Chromatic Scale—Four Notes per String

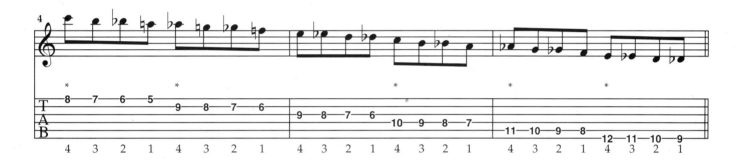

Chromatic Scale—Five Notes per String

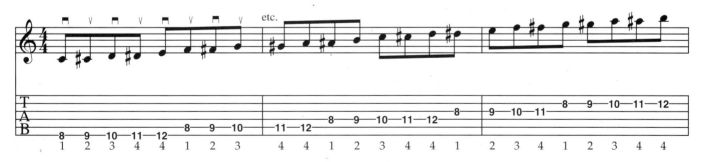

The Couch Potato Guitar Workout **39**

THE GREATEST GUITAR SCALES EVER: THE MAJOR AND MINOR PENTATONIC SCALES

At the risk of slightly overselling, the major and minor pentatonic scales are extremely helpful for improvising, learning more complex scales, and linking chord arpeggios and scales together. There are many ways to finger a pentatonic scale, but this section will focus on the sliding fingerings that alternate between two notes and three notes per string. By getting these fingerings into both your mind and muscle memory, you'll be well on your way to whizzing up and down the neck like a motocross racer—if that's your thing.

MAJOR PENTATONIC SCALE

First up is the *major pentatonic scale,* which is like a major scale without the 4th and 7th notes. Below is a one-octave fingering in the key of A. This fingering/fretboard pattern is the basis for the rest of this section. The scale degrees are labeled.

> **AND NOW, A WORD ABOUT SLIDES...**
>
> SL = *Shift slide.* Play the first note, then slide up or down to a second note on the same string and pick that note too.
>
> SL = *Legato slide.* Play the first note, then slide up or down to a second note on the same string. Only the first note is picked.

Major Pentatonic Scale in A, Root on String 6

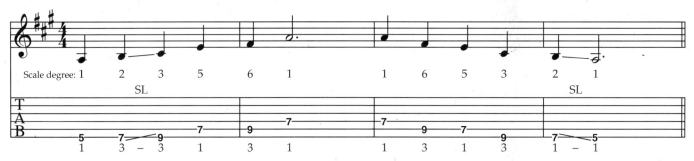

And now, let's play the scale one octave higher. Notice that it repeats the same fretboard pattern, but you have to shift up one extra fret when you go from string 3 to string 2. This is because these strings are tuned one half step closer together than the other strings. You'll have to keep this in mind anytime you are using a pattern that crosses between string 3 and string 2.

Major Pentatonic Scale in A, Root on String 4

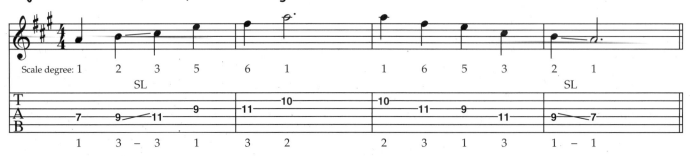

The following example shows a full three octaves.

Major Pentatonic Scale in A, Three Octaves

*Shift position for 4th finger

Once you can run up and down the three octaves and keep track of where you are, you can use the fingering at the bottom of page 40 as a basis for building scale patterns that will take you up the neck in a flurry of notes (without running out of notes too soon).

Here's one that incorporates a bend, triplets, hammer-ons, and pull-offs to get the most out of each octave of the scale. The musical idea in the first measure is repeated one octave higher in the second measure and then again one octave higher in the third measure. Use this as a template to create your own patterns.

"Three Octaves and a Cloud of Dust" Scale Run No. 1 (Ascending)

This one is a (more or less) descending run that uses a bit of sequencing and a bend. This is the kind of run that may remind you of The Allman Brothers Band or country-influenced picking.

"Three Octaves and a Cloud of Dust" Scale Run No. 2 (Descending)

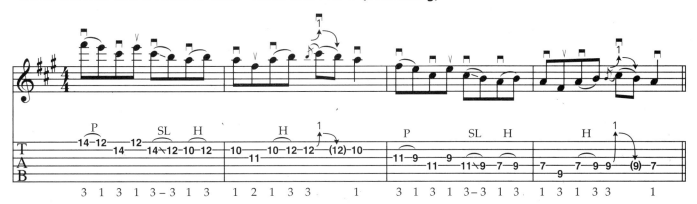

Before you move on, make sure you try this D Major Pentatonic fingering. It feels the same as the A Major Pentatonic, but it crosses over the 3rd and 2nd string at a different point in the pattern, so pay attention to avoid jumping the tracks.

Major Pentatonic Scale in D, Root on String 5

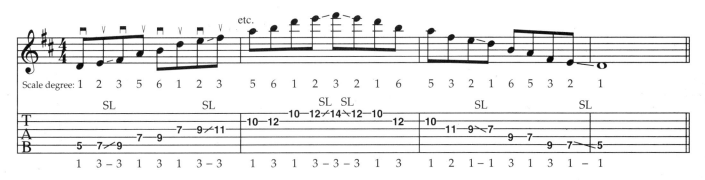

MINOR PENTATONIC SCALE

In the previous episode, you learned the major pentatonic sliding fingering. Now, due to a cruel and not-very-unexpected plot twist, you must learn the *minor pentatonic* sliding fingering.

The minor pentatonic contains the following scale degrees: 1-♭3-4-5-♭7. The fingering is actually the same fretboard pattern as the major pentatonic, but starts at a different point in the sequence of notes. It may help to think of the minor pentatonic as starting on finger 3, while the major pentatonic starts on finger 1. Notice that the pattern still alternates two notes on one string, then three notes on the next.

Minor Pentatonic Scale in A, Root on String 6

Now, let's play the scale one octave higher. Watch out for that position shift in the pattern when you get to the 2nd string.

Minor Pentatonic Scale in A, Root on String 4

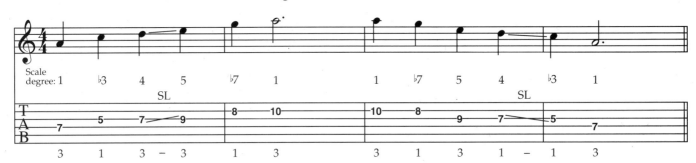

Below is the fingering strung together in nearly three octaves.

Minor Pentatonic in A, Almost Three Octaves

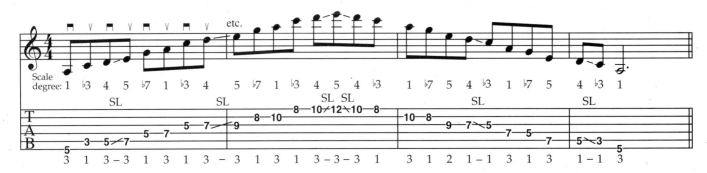

This is an ascending two-bar pattern that duplicates itself in two more octaves.

"Three Octaves and a Cloud of Dust" Scale Run No. 3 (Ascending)

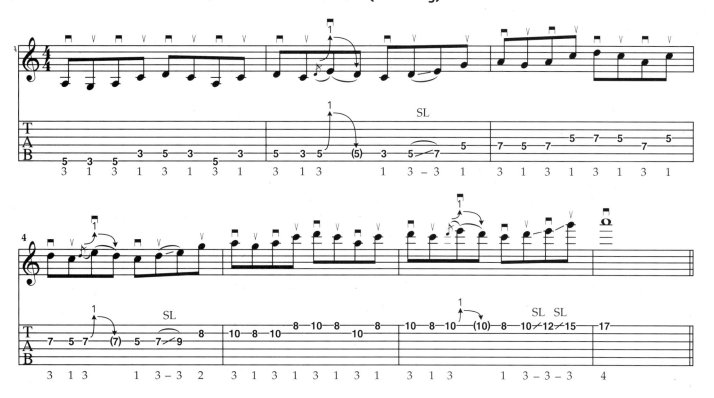

Here's a descending run.

"Three Octaves and a Cloud of Dust" Scale Run No. 4 (Descending)

Don't forget to see what happens when you start the scale pattern on string 5 instead of string 6.

Minor Pentatonic Scale in D, Root on String 5

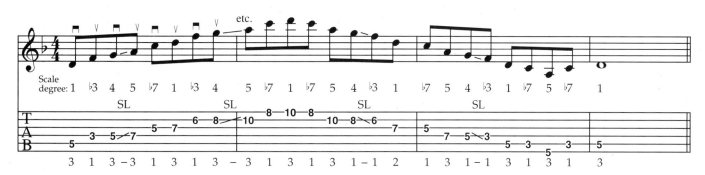

SPECIAL EFFECTS THAT BENEFIT
FROM MINDLESS COUCH PRACTICE

There are many kinds of practice situations, and there are many (many, many) things to practice. The trick is to match up the right practice goals to the right situations. If you're trying to take advantage of some time where it's too distracting to focus on music or compositional goals (like now, when you're on the couch reading and flicking popcorn at the cat), look for things to practice that are purely technical and need lots of time to develop. Here are a few examples.

VIBRATO

Vibrato is something you need in your playing. It represents your own unique and personal expressive voice on the instrument. Vibrato is a slight change in pitch on a particular note, where the change oscillates back and forth with the original note (or another change in pitch). Most styles of vibrato on the guitar are sharp, meaning the pitch change is made by bending or moving the string to make the note slightly sharp. A true vibrato is accomplished by raising and lowering the pitch of the note by an equal amount above and below the center pitch. You can only reliably accomplish this on a fretted guitar with either a tremolo/vibrato bar (whammy bar) or when you are playing with a slide.

Not everybody spends a lot of time practicing finger vibrato, because it is a complex muscle movement that develops slowly over time. This means you could practice it for five or ten minutes today and not necessarily notice that it's getting better, which is frustrating. Practice it every day for a couple of weeks, however, and you'll feel a change. Some player's signature sound takes years to develop.

Couch time is an ideal time to practice vibrato. Just practice moving the string on the fret with your left-hand fingers. It can actually be helpful to distract your conscious mind with the TV or the stereo while you do this. Make it a purely physical thing, just sit there and do it. Take away the demanding, goal-oriented part of your mind and just allow yourself to get used to the motion.

There are many techniques for vibrato, but they all involve moving the string against the fret, either up-and-down (as in string bending), or back-and-forth (which works better in the classical technique on nylon-string guitars). Watch your favorite players and imitate their techniques and sounds. Experiment with changing the width and speed of your vibrato. Soon, you'll develop your own collection of sounds to work into your playing.

TREMOLO PICKING

Even though the words *vibrato* and *tremolo* appear in similar places (like on amps or referring to whammy bars), *tremolo picking* refers to a right-hand technique. Tremolo picking is playing a single note (or chord) over and over very rapidly, like a machine gun. This technique is often associated with mandolin players, who have used rapid tremolo to overcome the instrument's lack of sustain since the old days in mother Italy. It's also a common technique in Spanish classical and flamenco guitar.

You can accomplish tremolo with a pick or with your right-hand fingers. Fingerstyle tremolo is a very complex motion, and requires explanation and training by a teacher to get the technique right. You can work on pick tremolo on your own. Just start picking a string using rapid alternating picking. Don't start too fast, because your goal is to maintain relaxation. If you see veins popping out of your arm, slow down and take a rest. You won't be able to keep that up for long.

As you work on your tremolo sound, try to keep the rhythm steady and the notes very even in volume. The idea is to eliminate those occasional clunky notes and misses, which distract from the overall effect. Pay attention to the balance of the pick in your hand, and try to keep the pick parallel to the string to keep the attacks of the downstrokes and upstrokes even.

As with vibrato, spend just a few minutes at a time on this and allow it to develop slowly over a long period. This is not about forcing a movement and powering through the wall. It's more about honing a motion to its most efficient, familiar, and relaxed state.

CHUGGING POWER CHORDS

If you play any rock, country, or blues guitar, then sooner or later you're going to find yourself chugging power chords with eighth-note downstrokes. Power chords are those two- or three-note root and 5th combos that are often used for rhythm playing on the low strings. Playing them with all downstrokes at too fast a speed can be fatiguing or cause your forearm to want to seize up. What's the solution? Couch potato practice!

The secret is relaxation and bounce. When you get faster, try to maintain the level of relaxation rather than forcing yourself into tightness. As your hand rebounds from hitting the strings, send it around in a tiny circle back towards the strings. Once again, time is on your side. Just bounce on the chord at a comfortable speed for a couple of minutes. Try it at a faster speed, then go back to the comfortable speed. Over time, your comfortable speed should increase. Think of it more like lightly dribbling a basketball and less like pounding nails.

THE COUCH POTATO FUNBOOK: IDEAS FOR INTERACTIVE PRACTICE

Why play a video game based on guitar players when you could just play a real guitar instead? Here are some suggestions for how to have a less zombie-like interaction with your friend the television. Of course, you could also turn off the TV and join a band, but that would be crazy.

COMPOSE AN INSTANT SOUNDTRACK

The most obvious use of your instrument while watching the tube is to make up a new soundtrack for the show. This can be difficult if the show is already full of music, but a little careful selection of programming can lead to a lot of fun.

Programs that have lots of empty space for your new soundtrack music:

- **Certain cop/detective shows:** Particularly ones with the words "Law" and "Order" in the title.

- **Old movies from the '30s and '40s:** Specifically, the less famous ones that didn't spend as much money on music.

- **Silent movies:** There are bands that go out to venues and perform live music to accompany silent movies. You can do this at home; there are still classic film channels that show silent films regularly.

- **Instructional programs:** Cooking and home improvement shows, hunting and fishing shows, and public educational programming all have wide open spaces that are just crying out for your musical genius.

- **News channels:** Seriously, what news program couldn't be improved by your musical commentary?

- **Soap operas, courtroom shows, afternoon talk shows:** The list goes on and on...

Soundtracks are full of elements that are suited to specific types of situations. Here are some of the soundtrack elements you could work into your playing.

- **Stingers:** These are chords or themes that punctuate moments of excitement. Stingers are a great way to practice new or weird chords, and can make a show much funnier or scarier than it is.

- **Transitions/bumpers:** This is the music that is used to get from scene to scene, or to play the show out to a commercial break. Hit the mute button early, and be the band!

- **Leitmotifs:** Back in the big opera days, composers such as Wagner would write short themes for each character to capture their essence in music and introduce them when they came on stage. These themes are called *leitmotifs* (pronounced like "light mow teef"). Writing leitmotifs for characters can be a particularly fun way to interact with otherwise soul-crushing reality shows.

- **Chase scenes:** Even though there's already music in the soundtrack, it is often just drums and bass lines, leaving you lots of room to solo or groove. Of course, you'll have to figure out what key the music is in, which must be done by using your ear to first determine the root note—the note on your guitar that seems strongest, or seems to best match the music in the soundtrack. This will take some trial and error and some searching, but, with time and practice, you will improve. Next, you have to determine if the key is major or minor. Starting on the root note, try a minor pentatonic scale and then a major pentatonic scale. The one that doesn't seem to clash with the soundtrack is the one to use.

"HI BOB"—THE GUITAR EDITION

Way back in the 1970s, there was a wildly popular TV show called "The Bob Newhart Show." The show's popularity in reruns spawned an impromptu parlor game known as "Hi Bob." Whenever anybody greeted Mr. Newhart on the show with the words "Hi Bob," viewers would take a sip of their favorite beverage (an herbal tea or a cranberry spritzer perhaps).

You could adapt this game to the instrument and save yourself a fortune in swizzle sticks. Just take your favorite show and pick out a catch phrase. Whenever it is uttered by a character on the show, the first person in the room to dash off a searing face-melter of a musical run wins the round. For example, if you're watching a home improvement show, you could play a lick every time somebody says, "dated cabinets." You'll get a lot of practice this way.

IMITATION GAMES

Here are some games that you can only play when you're the only person in the house. This will be so irritating to your friends and family (unless they are all avant-garde musicians) that you may become homeless if you try this when they're around. These games are great for freeing you up from physical habits and giving new inspiration to your music.

The object of the game is to imitate what you hear or see on the screen. Here are some variations:

- **Ear-training imitation:** Anytime you hear a bit of music on a TV show, try to play it back right after you hear it. You could try to get it as correct as possible, or just imitate the basic musical shape and attitude of the thing. The more correctly you can reproduce it, the more you are training your ears for melody, harmony, and rhythm.

- **Speech imitation:** As you watch a show or movie, try to imitate the speech of the characters with your instrument. Imitate the rhythms, the rises and falls of pitch and inflection, the intensity of emotion. This is especially fun if you're watching something that would be mind-numbingly stupid if you weren't covering up all the dialog with your playing.

- **Improvisation from visual inspiration:** Try to interpret the action on the screen by playing your instrument. This is not quite the same as coming up with an instant soundtrack. This improv exercise will probably sound much wilder and weirder. If someone is strolling, play your idea of "strolling." If you see someone chopping zucchini, interpret that on the instrument. Alternatively, you could try to imitate the emotions of characters, or even the colors and lighting that the director has used.

CONCLUSION

As you have discovered, there are many ways to take advantage of your vegging-out time in front of the TV. These times are actually perfect opportunities to work on and develop technical skills that might otherwise be a bit tedious to work on if your mind wasn't occupied by something else. As mentioned in the Introduction, many of the exercises in this book require some preparation. It might take you a little time to learn a new pattern or technique. But once you get it down, it will take very little thought to sit there and noodle away—building your speed, agility, and finger independence while staying caught up on your favorite TV shows. Hey, you're also spending quality time with the person (or persons) at the other end of the couch (maybe not so much...). Anyway, the point is, it's not always a bad thing to be a couch potato. Have some fun learning your instrument; there are opportunities for growth and development in places you least expect!